Not of This World

What a True Believer Looks Like

A. Gilbert Ybarra

renownpublishing

Renown Publishing
www.renownpublishing.com

Not of This World / A. Gilbert Ybarra
ISBN-13: 978-1-952602-12-2

This book is not mere theory; it was forged in joy, adversity, and everyday life and aged over years of faithful discipleship. Pastor Ybarra shares a blueprint for healthy, victorious living. "This is the way, walk ye in it" (Isaiah 30:21 KJV).

James B. Shelton | *Professor of New Testament* | *Oral Roberts University*

Gilbert has a heart for people and a passion for God's word. *Not of This World* helps every believer walk victoriously while in this world. What a great tool for discipleship and spiritual growth!

Randy Robison | *LIFE Today TV*

To my wife, Fannie. Thank you for your endurance and unwavering commitment through the ups and downs of our lives together, serving the Lord.

To my children—Andrew, Victoria-Lauren, Christian, and Alexandria. I am proud of you and thank the Lord for each of you.

To the Savior of the world. Thank You, Jesus, for all You have done and all You continue to do for us.

CONTENTS

You Are Not of This World

...but as he who called you is holy, you also be holy in all your conduct, since it is written, "You shall be holy, for I am holy."

—1 Peter 1:15–16 *(ESV)*

There is a crisis in the world today. What used to be sacred and holy is now politically incorrect and appalling. Right has become wrong, and wrong has become right. Purity is considered outdated and irrelevant since it has become acceptable to prevent or abort unwanted pregnancies. How far we have fallen from God's plan and standard in our nation!

Sadly, even the church has blurred the lines between righteousness and sin. It has become difficult to distinguish any difference in behavior between a believer and a nonbeliever. They act, dress, and talk the same. Christians and non-Christians go to the same dives with abandon, unconcerned with holy living. They listen to the same music and value the same entertainment. The pressure has never been greater to affirm all lifestyles, no matter how ungodly and unhealthy they may be. It has become fashionable, even among believers, to accept the standards of the world rather than standing up for biblical values. It is gauche to offend anyone—except God.

While many Christians don't even try to be different, there are some who *do* try, but insincerely. They look, dress, and talk the part, but they are wolves in sheep's clothing (Matthew 7:15). Their toxic behavior can misrepresent the whole church, hurting other believers, setting the wrong example for new converts, and sending the wrong message to nonbelievers. A true believer is different from both examples.

So, what does God want from you? There are clear directions in His Word.

> But you are a chosen people, a royal priesthood, a holy nation, God's special possession, that you may declare the praises of him who called you out of darkness into his wonderful light.
> —*1 Peter 2:9*

Why has He called you to be holy? You are to be an example, to believers and nonbelievers alike, and to praise "him who called you out of darkness." Holiness manifests in love for God that overwhelms any fear of others' opinions. Though if you think that holiness means keeping a long face and never having fun, consider that Jesus said:

> If you keep my commands, you will remain in my love, just as I have kept my Father's commands and remain in his love. I have told you this so that my joy may be in you and that your joy may be complete.
> —*John 15:10–11*

You are in this world, but not of it (John 15:19; John 17:14–16). While many today will call this antiquated theology—too religious, too legalistic, too narrow-minded—the Bible has not changed. Believing and obeying the Word of God is the foundation of a Christian life.

What do true believers look like? What are their habits? What are the core principles of their beliefs? How do they act and react to the people and events around them? What decisions do they make when no one else is looking? What fruit do they produce on a regular basis?

In this book, I will address seven core characteristics of a true believer. We'll explore how a fervent Christian:

1. Praises and worships God, both privately and corporately.

2. Has a consistent, regular devotional life.

3. Regularly bears the fruit of the Spirit.

4. Abstains from and avoids the lusts of the flesh.

5. Maintains fellowship with other believers.

6. Shares his or her faith and disciples other Christians.

7. Gives time, resources, and finances to further the work of God.

Application-focused workbook sections will supplement each chapter and help you to develop these attributes in your life.

For many, these seven characteristics will be new. For others, this book can serve as a reset button, moving them from a crooked path to a straight one. You will be able to identify any bad fruit in your own life and in the lives of others who may try to influence you wrongly. Most of all, this book provides a guideline for avoiding the pitfalls and mindsets of the secular world in which we live.

Bring an open mind and heart to God and allow Him to speak to you so that your walk can be deeper and more meaningful than it has ever been. Set yourself apart to spend your life faithfully serving Jesus.

The goal of this book is not necessarily to bring attention to the way people dress or the activities in which they participate. Instead, it is about examining the condition of the heart.

> *The LORD does not look at the things people look at. People look at the outward appearance, but the LORD looks at the heart.*
>
> **—1 Samuel 16:7b**

We shouldn't take the principles laid out in this book and become holiness police over the lives of others. This book is designed for examining our own lives, actions, and reactions and the condition of our own hearts. The principles and characteristics laid out in the next few chapters are good indicators of how true believers should conduct their lives.

CHAPTER ONE

Praise and Worship God

...always giving thanks to God the Father for everything, in the name of our Lord Jesus Christ.
—Ephesians 5:20

The Lord draws you to praise and worship Him. Something happens when you participate in praise and worship. The atmosphere changes. The spirit realm is activated. Though it may take time to develop, praise and worship must become part of your everyday life. It may be against our nature to do so, but making a conscious decision and commitment to worship is fundamental in the daily walk of a true believer.

Now, there's a line between continual worship and being weird, unapproachable, and disconnected from others. Don't be so heavenly minded that you're no earthly good. But keep your heart and mind open for those interludes when it is possible to connect with your Maker, and the rest will fall into place.

Ephesians 5:20 says, "...always giving thanks to God the Father for everything, in the name of our Lord Jesus Christ"—not sometimes for some things, but all the time for everything. First Thessalonians 5:18 says to "...give thanks in all circumstances; for this is God's will for you in Christ Jesus"—not when things are just perfect, but in all circumstances. Should you rejoice in the Lord sometimes or just when things are going well? No, we are told to rejoice in the Lord *always*!

True believers praise and worship God under two conditions: when they feel like it and when they don't. Of course, it's not hard to praise God when everything is fine. Your mortgage or rent is paid, your kids are in perfect health, and everyone in your family is serving God.

But if you get a doctor's report with bad news or you can't pay your water bill, if you are a true believer, you will still give thanks and worship the Lord. Amid life's challenges and with havoc and godlessness in the news daily—*in spite* of this—a believer will worship the Lord.

When you're heartbroken, you may feel like it doesn't make sense to worship God. You may think, "What is there to worship Him for when I am in pain?" But at that moment, God is worthy of all your praise and your utmost devotion (Psalm 96:4). Amazingly, something begins to shift in you as you start worshipping God in the midst of the storm. You begin to feel His presence and experience the joy of trusting Him.

What an amazing moment! Everything inside you tells you to scream, to cave in, to panic and give up, but you choose to worship God instead. Praise and worship in the most difficult moments of life can seem daunting, even impossible. But God often feels closer in these moments than most other times in life.

Cause to Worship

In her compelling book *The Hiding Place*, Corrie ten Boom related such a realization.[1] She and her sister Betsie were imprisoned in Ravensbrück Concentration Camp during World War II. They had been caught hiding Jews in their Holland home during the Nazi occupation.

When Corrie and Betsie arrived in the crowded, filthy women's barracks, Corrie panicked. Fleas! Everywhere! How could they possibly live in such a place?

Betsie was undaunted, reminding Corrie of the words of 1 Thessalonians: to rejoice, to pray without ceasing, and to give thanks in all circumstances. What could they possibly be thankful for in a Nazi-run extermination camp? Betsie named a few things:

- They were together.

- They were in a barracks crammed with women, so more could hear them teach about God.

- The guards hadn't found their Bible when they were stripped of their belongings.

- And the fleas.

That's where Corrie drew the line. No, she couldn't—she wouldn't—be thankful for the fleas! But Betsie insisted, and eventually Corrie thanked God for the painful little pests as well.

As time went on, they continued studying the Word day after day in their barracks, unimpeded by the guards. The women couldn't imagine why no one came to break up their meetings. One day, Betsie learned the truth. The guards wouldn't set foot in a room full of fleas. Our God is so big! Even under the most extreme conditions, He intervenes. The Lord uses even the lowliest of His creatures for our good.

In the book of 1 Kings, there is another account of God using unusual creatures, this time to provide for the prophet Elijah in the wilderness. Elijah had just announced that a great drought would befall Israel, and he was hiding away from King Ahab, who was not too pleased with the news. Doubtless, Ahab would kill Elijah if he found him.

> Then the word of the LORD came to Elijah: "Leave here, turn eastward and hide in the Kerith Ravine, east of the Jordan. You will drink from the brook, and I have directed the ravens to supply you with food there."
>
> So he did what the LORD had told him. He went to the Kerith Ravine, east of the Jordan, and stayed there. The ravens brought him bread and meat in the morning and bread and meat in the evening, and he drank from the brook.
> **—1 Kings 17:2–6**

Now, the raven has not had the best press for the most part. Normally feeding on carrion, the raven was associated with death and the unclean in ancient Israel. Jews were strictly forbidden to eat them, and ravens probably had very bad breath. Nevertheless, God sent ravens to feed Elijah. Ravens had the perfect skills to get the job done.

Don't ever discount God's willingness and ability to rescue you from your dilemma. All of nature responds to His command, and if He did it for Elijah, He can do it for you, regardless of how impossible it may seem!

Trusting Him Through Worship

King David declared in Psalm 44:6–8, "I put no trust in my bow, my sword does not bring me victory; but you give us victory over our enemies, you put our adversaries to shame. In God we make our boast all day long, and we will praise your name forever." When you praise and worship God, especially when it doesn't make sense, you declare that your trust is not in your "bow" or your "weapon." It's in God.

Of course, most people today don't carry around weapons of war to protect themselves from their enemies. It is more likely that you are tempted to trust in your own abilities, talents, finances, intellect, connections, or other resources in daily life rather than submitting to God. Through worship, especially in difficult circumstances, you're showing that your trust lies solely in the Lord. The solutions to your life challenges come totally from the Lord. As you practice this trust and make it a lifestyle, you take the focus off of yourself and place it on God.

I remember when I was in the middle of a crisis early in the life of our church. We had overextended ourselves in putting on, of all things, a praise and worship event. We were about $2,000 in debt and didn't have the money to pay it off. We had no idea where we would get the funds. I felt enormous pressure.

I had a decision to make. I could quit, blame God, curse my own life, fret and worry, even lock myself in a room and cry myself to sleep, or I could do the exact opposite of what I wanted to do: I could praise and worship God. Despite the flesh wanting to do everything but worship God, I did what I knew I had to do. It did not take long for the Father to lift my anxiety, and my praise and worship began to fill the atmosphere. Right there in my van, while driving home by myself, I worshipped the Lord. My focus shifted from my problems, my shortcomings, and my situation to how awesome God is and what a mighty God I serve. It was such an intimate moment with God, just He and I.

I began to realize that my life was not my own (1 Corinthians 6:19–20). I belonged to Him. As the pressure began to melt away, my anxiety turned to joy and a hunger to serve God. I was not worried at all, even though I still had no idea how I was going to get the money. I knew that our great God was in control. The outcome didn't matter. With my focus on God, paying the bills no longer seemed important. Basking in the presence of the Lord was all I needed at that moment.

I didn't know where I was going to get $2,000. That amount of money was out of my reach. But after worshipping God, I knew that I was His child and He would supply whatever I needed (Philippians 4:19). Period.

When I stopped by my mailbox on the way home, I found a letter addressed to me from another church. It contained a check for $2,000. I was totally overwhelmed by the glory of the moment. It was clear to me then that money was never the issue. The Lord just wanted my love and trust. He wanted me to be at peace in His presence. When I was tempted to worry about the money, He had already provided it for me. It was waiting for me in my mailbox. Trusting that He would provide during uncertainty enabled me to stay at peace while I waited.

You serve a mighty God who cares for you. Praise Him in all circumstances and worship Him for who He is, in the good times and especially in the bad. Understanding and practicing this will change your life, your ministry, and your family.

Where Do You Worship?

Worship is both private and communal. Many Christians think that praise and worship is just for twenty minutes at the beginning of a Sunday service. This is important, but it is not meant to be the only time and place for worship. Privately, when no one is looking, you can express your love in ways you never would in public: dancing, singing off-key, lying prostrate on the floor, shouting—you fill in the blank. Some of my most intimate and meaningful times of praise and worship came when it was just God and I.

Sometimes there is conflict in your home. Peace may

be the last thing on anyone's mind. Mom and Dad are frustrated, and the kids have nothing better to do than to get on each other's last nerve. I challenge you to put on praise and worship music at that moment. Blast it through your speakers until it fills the whole house. You will be shocked by the difference this makes in your home. Make worship practical, a gift of submission, at all times, everywhere. You will soon find that you stop telling God how big your mountain is and start telling your mountain how big your God is![2]

In Deuteronomy 9:1–6, we see that the children of Israel had the daunting task of facing the Anakim army in battle at Jericho as they crossed into the promised land. The Anakim were warriors. They were not only literal giants; they knew how to fight. They were organized and powerful, and they had large cities with "walls up to the sky" (Deuteronomy 9:1). No way could the Israelites stand against them! But God could, and He delivered His people.

The Lord told Joshua:

> On the seventh day, march around the city seven times, with the priests blowing the trumpets. When you hear them sound a long blast on the trumpets, have the whole army give a loud shout; then the wall of the city will collapse and the army will go up, everyone straight in.
> —Joshua 6:4b–5

The giant warriors were protected by a wall that towered into the sky, yet God instructed all of the Israelites to shout with a voice of triumph. He instructed them to shout with victory, even before the battle had begun.

The Hebrew word translated as "shout" here is *ruwa*, which means to shout with a voice of triumph.[3] After reading that, I now shout, *"Ruwa!"* when I encounter troubles that seem to reach to the sky, and I imagine them tumbling to the ground in little pieces. This is prophetic praise. In other words, I praise the Lord in advance for the breakthrough He will bring. Though you may not see the solution in that moment, choose to worship Him as though you already have the victory.

When you face giants in your life—and you will—it may seem that the odds are stacked against you. Whatever the challenge, it invariably is greater than your endurance, your bank account, your medical insurance, your income, your ability, and your talents. Victory appears impossible.

The enemy whispers in your ear, reminding you of your past failures and doing his best to convince you that you don't stand a chance to win the battle. Don't be swayed by his lies. God is much bigger and greater than any circumstance or situation. God's promises are true, and you can stand on those promises. Use praise and worship as an offensive weapon. Shout, *"Ruwa!"*—just as the Israelites did before their triumph at Jericho.

This is not a random shout without purpose. It is a shout that confuses the enemy. It is a God kind of shout. It is a shout that moves the heavenlies into action. Anticipate your victory. Praise and worship God not only for what He has done, but also for what He is going to do, as if victory were already yours.

Additionally, this stance of praise keeps you in a place of joy and peace while you wait to see the unfolding of God's provision for your circumstances. Rather than being weighed down by worry and anxiety, you can rest easy, knowing that help is on the way. As Jesus said, "Can any one of you by worrying add a single hour to your life?" (Matthew 6:27).

was always open to the Lord and His correction. He wanted to please and obey God.

David wrote many songs found in the book of Psalms that expressed his love for God in worship and praise.

I will praise you, LORD, with all my heart; before the "gods" I will sing your praise. I will bow down toward your holy temple and will praise your name....
—Psalm 138:1–2a

Come, let us sing for joy to the LORD; let us shout aloud to the Rock of our salvation. Let us come before him with thanksgiving and extol him with music and song.
—Psalm 95:1–2

I will exalt you, my God the King; I will praise your name for ever and ever. Every day I will praise you and extol your name for ever and ever. Great is the LORD and most worthy of praise; his greatness no one can fathom.
—Psalm 145:1–3

My mouth will speak in praise of the LORD. Let every creature praise his holy name for ever and ever.
—Psalm 145:21

I will praise the LORD at all times. I will constantly speak his praises.
—Psalm 34:1 (NLT)

Before moving on to the next chapter, take a few

moments to choose one of David's prayers and pray it as your own.

WORKBOOK

Chapter One Questions

Question: When is it easiest for you to praise God? When is it most challenging? What are some ways you can worship even in the midst of grief, fear, or other overwhelming emotions?

_____

_____

_____

_____

_____

_____

_____

_____

_____

_____

_____

_____

Question: Why is it so important to praise God when you don't feel like it and when your circumstances look hopeless? How will an attitude of worship help the situation even if God does not change the circumstances?

_____

_____

_____

_____

_____

_____

_____

_____

_____

_____

_____

Question: What are the benefits of private worship? What are the benefits of corporate worship? How are you prioritizing both in your life?

_____

_____

_____

_____

_____

_____

_____

_____

_____

_____

_____

_____

_____

Action: Study an example from Scripture of a great breakthrough or victory that followed faith-filled praise (for instance, King Jehoshaphat in battle in 2 Chronicles 20, David facing the Amalekites in 1 Samuel 30, or Paul and Silas in the Philippian jail in Acts 16). What was the crisis? How did God's people worship, and what was the result?

_____

_____

_____

_____

_____

_____

_____

_____

_____

_____

_____

Action: Describe a time when you have praised God amid difficult circumstances, in spite of your natural inclinations. How did it feel to praise God in that moment? What were the results of your situation?

_____

_____

_____

_____

_____

_____

_____

_____

_____

_____

Chapter One Notes

_____

_____

_____

_____

_____

_____

_____

_____

_____

_____

_____

_____

_____

_____

_____

_____

_____

_____

_____

_____

_____

_____

CHAPTER TWO

Pray and Read the Word

Jesus went out as usual to the Mount of Olives, and his disciples followed him.

—Luke 22:39

Jesus was the anointed one of God, the Messiah, the Savior of mankind. Even so, He did not start a day without communing with His Father for sustenance, instruction, and power. He said, "Very truly I tell you, the Son can do nothing by himself; he can do only what he sees his Father doing, because whatever the Father does the Son also does. For the Father loves the Son and shows him all he does" (John 5:19–20a).

How did Jesus learn what the Father was doing? He went to the mountains to pray. He loved talking to the Father, and He experienced the Father's love in return. Prayer is vital. Prayer is life-giving. Prayer unleashes God's power on earth.

In order to grow into Jesus' likeness, you must pursue the Father's heart and mind through daily devotions, just as Jesus did. Christians who do not have a regular devotional life miss out on the awesome fruit of time alone with God. Prayer and Scripture study are not duties.

They are your lifeline. If you want to hear God's voice, if you want peace, wisdom, faith for healing, and salvation for your loved ones, then pray. If you want to serve the Lord with your whole heart, soul, mind, and strength (Mark 12:30), then pray and read God's Word endlessly.

Jesus said, "Whoever wants to be my disciple must deny themselves and take up their cross daily and follow me" (Luke 9:23). Spending time with God is a sacrifice of mind and body as you focus on Him alone. Prayer is more essential than anything else we do. In the book of Luke, Jesus commended Mary for sitting at His feet instead of being preoccupied with serving:

> *"Martha, Martha," the Lord answered, "you are worried and upset about many things, but few things are needed— or indeed only one. Mary has chosen what is better, and it will not be taken away from her."*
> **—Luke 10:41–42**

Healthy devotional lives are rare in the church today. As a result, many Christians are self-serving rather than God-pleasing. We become more interested in fulfilling our agenda than God's. How healthy is your devotional life? You know that you should read your Bible and pray, but do you? Perhaps you think that it's not very important, so you give priority to other issues in your life. Certainly, there are many other things to claim your attention. Some are even legitimate. But think about it. All of God's servants in Scripture prayed: Moses, David, Joseph, Daniel, John, Mary, Paul, Anna. The list goes on and on. In fact, if you want a challenging research project, try to find even one who did not.

A Healthy Diet of Prayer

Everyone on earth understands the importance of eating food and drinking water. These things are necessary to sustain life. If you don't eat or drink on a consistent basis, you become malnourished. If that condition continues, it will lead to death. It is the same for the spirit of a believer. Prolonged starvation from lack of prayer and devotion can lead to spiritual death.

If the flesh (or fleshly desire) dominates an individual, that person is on the wide path leading to destruction (Matthew 7:13). When the Spirit dominates, the path leads to Jesus. A strong devotional life is critical to walking in the Spirit and developing His fruit.

If you only eat once a week or once a month, I can guarantee that you won't be healthy. You can stuff yourself in one sitting, but it is still unhealthy and dangerous to skip food for the rest of the week. The same is true for your devotional life. If you believe that it's okay to devote your life to God only once a week, then your spiritual life will be unbalanced and unhealthy.

When I was a young Christian, I used to ask my brothers in Christ, "What would your spirit look like if you could see it right now? Would it look like a healthy bodybuilder, or would it look like a half-starved wimp suffering from malnutrition because you don't pray or read the Bible?"

Someone who works out and exercises daily finds it easier to move, walk, and balance. He or she will be stronger and have more energy than someone who rarely or never exercises. People who never exercise will be listless, unable to take long walks or lift heavy objects. Daily exercise for thirty minutes is more effective than working out for three hours once a week. The same is true for our spiritual devotional life. It is more important and fruitful to have a regular thirty-minute daily devotional time than to have one three-hour session per week.

For physical training is of some value, but godliness has value for all things, holding promise for both the present life and the life to come.
                                            —1 Timothy 4:8

Daily Prayer, Daily Blessings

The Bible is clear that our Christian walk is a daily walk. Not a weekly walk. Not a once-in-a-while walk. The Bible says that we are to carry our cross daily, as we see in the passage from Luke when Jesus went to pray "as usual" (Luke 22:39). We read in many different places that it was customary for Jesus to withdraw from people and pray (Luke 5:16; Mark 1:35). He would go to a place where He could get alone with His Father and seek His face.

When Jesus taught His disciples how to pray, He asked God to "give us today our daily bread" (Matthew 6:9–13). The key word here is *daily*. No one would ask for stale bread once a week. You eat daily, and you should pray daily. God's "great love" is "new every morning" (Lamentations 3:22–23). Prayer is like a morning shower that will clean and refresh you as you get ready for the day.

Jesus said:

Therefore I tell you, whatever you ask for in prayer, believe that you have received it, and it will be yours.
                                            —Mark 11:24

Watch and pray so that you will not fall into temptation. The spirit is willing, but the flesh is weak.

—Mark 14:38

Prayer strengthens your spirit.

Is it hard to pray? Yes, many times it is. You will go through seasons of excitement when every prayer seems the most effective one you could utter. Then there will be times when every word falls to the floor and God Himself seems bored.

A frenetic schedule and daily responsibilities can challenge your commitment and overshadow your spiritual walk. It takes discipline and a purposeful heart to pursue this precious time with God. Life happens, and there may be times when it is impossible to keep your set devotion time. You can be flexible if you need to be, but committing to being consistent in your devotional time with God will be life-giving. Even if you miss a day or two, dust yourself off and start again.

The Power of Prayer

Speaking the Word of God over your life through prayer is the most powerful weapon you have in your spiritual arsenal. You should take full advantage of it. When prayer is the key to seeking God's heart, why neglect it? When prayer is key to keeping you humble, why deny praying to Him? Prayer moves the hand of God.

It is time to wake up and smell the coffee. You need to pray and read the Word of God. Excuses only work against you. You may not be called to preach or have a pulpit ministry, but you *are* called to pray. Even Jesus said, "*When* you pray," not "*If* you pray" (Luke 11:2; Matthew 6:5–6; emphasis added). No one is greater than his or her prayer life.

Paul wrote that we should "pray without ceasing" (1 Thessalonians 5:17 ESV). Pray continually, without ceasing. Establish a solid, consistent prayer life. Pray in secret. Set aside a place free from distractions that remind you of all the things you have yet to do in the day, a place where no one else can eavesdrop and inhibit your conversation. Then just talk to your Father. Prayer is personal.

Jesus said:

> And when you pray, do not be like the hypocrites, for they love to pray standing in the synagogues and on the street corners to be seen by others. Truly I tell you, they have received their reward in full. But when you pray, go into your room, close the door and pray to your Father, who is unseen. Then your Father, who sees what is done in secret, will reward you.
>
> —*Matthew 6:5–6*

Prayer is not a showy fruit. Who will ever know whether you pray regularly or not? But prayer changes things. God has made you into His partner, choosing to work through you as you pray for the will of God to be accomplished on earth. You're His partner, so pray!

Meditating on the Word Daily

> Blessed is the one who does not walk in step with the wicked or stand in the way that sinners take or sit in the company of mockers, but whose delight is in the law of the LORD, and who meditates on his law day and night. That person is like a tree planted by streams of water, which yields its fruit in season and whose leaf does not wither— whatever they do prospers.
>
> —*Psalm 1:1–3*

Daily devotional reading and meditating on Scripture leads to a believer producing fruit. Reading the Word of God is life-sustaining to the true believer as water is to a tree. According to Jesus, everyone who drinks from the water He provides will never thirst again (John 4:13–14). You will be like a tree planted by a stream. When the heat and trials come, whether from nature, happenstance, or our own actions, the enemy is always waiting to get a foot in the door. However, consuming the Word daily helps to sustain and prosper us in these situations.

One day, I woke up and could hear what sounded like the hissing and static of a radio stuck between stations. I didn't think much of it when I heard this same thing just after waking up the next few days. Then I realized that we didn't have a radio. What was I hearing?

I went to the doctor, and they told me that I had tinnitus. I had never heard of this before, but I knew that I wanted it to be gone. The problem was that there wasn't really a cure. The best I could do was try to minimize the symptoms with my diet.

Though it may not seem that dire, I can't express how my prognosis made me feel. At the time, you would have thought that they had handed me a death sentence. To make matters worse, a co-worker told me that there were cases of people committing suicide because of the ringing in their ears.

The next year was miserable for me. I thought that I would go insane. I prayed and prayed, but the ringing would not go away.

After a while, I started to declare the Word of God over my life. I was desperate for relief. Over and over I would say, "For God has not given us a spirit of fear, but of power and of love and of a sound mind" (2 Timothy 1:7 NKJV).

This didn't immediately solve my problem, but I began to feel hopeful about my situation. God brought peace to me. Twenty years later, I still have ringing in my ears, but the Word of God has sustained me throughout that time. My leaves did not wither and die in the heat.

Developing a Devotional Life

In an unhealthy relationship, people never communicate, or only one person does all the talking. When disaster strikes, this relationship will fall apart. You do not want that to describe your relationship with the Father. Here are some practical suggestions to keep the lines of communication open:

- Set aside a little time each day for reading the Bible and praying.

- Find a quiet place. You can even have your phone or tablet read Scripture to you on your way to work.

- Read a devotional (there are thousands for free online), write in a journal, and talk to God.

- Not sure what to say? Start with thanking God and praising Him for who He is. Try reading a psalm for inspiration.

- Confess your sin.

- Think about the areas of your life that feel dry and empty. Ask for wisdom and new life in those areas.

Then watch as your knowledge and love for God grow. Life changes as you humble yourself and commune with God. His presence will wash over you. His Book will fill your heart and mind with unspeakable treasures. That's a promise.

Oh, the depth of the riches of the wisdom and knowledge of God! How unsearchable his judgments, and his paths beyond tracing out! "Who has known the mind of the Lord? Or who has been his counselor?" "Who has ever given to God, that God should repay them?" For from him and through him and for him are all things. To him be the glory forever! Amen.

—Romans 11:33–36

Jesus did not leave us orphans when He ascended into heaven; He promised an Advocate to live inside us and guide us to all truth (John 14:16–18, 26; John 16:13). In the next chapter, you will see the kind of fruit that can be borne out of spending time with God and walking in His Spirit. The Holy Spirit makes the impossible possible, and you become a new creation in Christ (2 Corinthians 5:17).

WORKBOOK

Chapter Two Questions

Question: In what ways is a devotional life like food? How can it be compared to exercise? What hinders you from spending time with God daily?

_____

_____

_____

_____

_____

_____

_____

_____

_____

_____

Question: What are some of the blessings that come only through prayer? What do you find difficult about prayer? How can you be persistent in prayer through a challenging season?

_____

_____

_____

_____

_____

_____

_____

_____

_____

_____

_____

Question: Describe a relationship in which you and another person slowly drifted apart because of a lack of communication. What caused the silence? How can you prevent that from happening in your relationship with God? How do you listen to God?

_____

_____

_____

_____

_____

_____

_____

_____

_____

_____

_____

Question: What things should you profess or declare with (greater) conviction? What things should you cease to declare?

_____

_____

_____

_____

_____

_____

_____

_____

_____

_____

Action: Make a plan to start a devotional time. When will you do it and for how long? With what passage in the Bible will you start? Will you also read a devotional book or use a phone app? Will you use a prayer system or list? Will you journal? If the idea of having devotions seems overwhelming, ask a Christian friend who is faithful in this discipline to give you some pointers. If you are already faithful, encourage a younger or new believer to begin and stay consistent in daily devotions.

Chapter Two Notes

_____

_____

_____

_____

_____

_____

_____

_____

_____

_____

_____

_____

_____

_____

_____

_____

_____

_____

CHAPTER THREE

Walk in the Spirit

Each tree is recognized by its own fruit. People do not pick figs from thornbushes, or grapes from briers.
—Luke 6:44

Expectation of Blessings

A man marched into a bank, chin high, eyes focused straight ahead, a piece of paper clutched in his hand. He crossed the marble floor in a straight line to a teller behind brass bars. Slapping the paper on the counter, he slid it across to the teller.

With a bored expression, the teller glanced at the slip. His brow rose as deft fingers tapped several numbers into a keyboard. "A withdrawal for one hundred thousand dollars?"

The man tapped the counter with his fingernail. "I'm in a hurry."

"I'm sure you are," the teller answered. "But it looks as if you'll be waiting quite some time. You've only got $15.98 in your account."

"You must be mistaken."

"No, sir." The clerk drew his hands together. "It is you who are mistaken. We don't make mistakes."

The man leaned forward, grasped the bars, and yelled, "I don't care what my account says! I know you have the money here, and I want it now!"

"Sir, please keep your voice down. This is a bank, and because of many oversight audits, I can confidently say that you only have…."

The man looked to the sky and raised his voice to the elegantly painted ceiling. "Such a greedy bank. I want the money!"

Guards reached for their holsters.

The man pointed to a woman in front of a nearby teller. "You!"

She clutched at her purse as the man yelled, "You took the money!"

Guards encircled him. "Time to go," one of the guards said as they escorted the man from the bank.

As unlikely as this story sounds, it demonstrates what people sometimes expect from life: a free pass for un-earned riches, good fruit from an untended tree. Reality is quite different. You must put some money into your bank account if you expect to take it out later!

Good Seed

The man who plants a watermelon seed shouldn't ex-pect corn to grow. It's a simple thought, but also a profound one. You can't plant bad seeds and get good crops. Even if you plant good seeds, they need to be nur-tured in order to grow properly. It only takes a quick glance at a tomato patch to tell who waters, fertilizes, and weeds their plants and who doesn't.

What is the crop you are looking for here, the "fruit" that Christians talk about? It is your behavior and its effect on others. It is your response to suffering. It is what you say and the way you carry yourself. It is God's love made visible and tangible. It is maturity of character, developed over time, that makes you look like Jesus.

If you plant bad seeds or ignore destructive pests that devour your plants, your fruit and subsequent seeds will be rotten, no good to anyone, and disgusting to keep in the house. But if you work hard so that the roots of your character grow strong and deep and can weather any storm, your fruit will grow well and continue to reproduce through healthy seeds.

Roots Determine Fruit

Trees are very large plants, so they have strong roots that branch out and spread far and wide. The roots anchor the tree and extract moisture and nutrients from the soil. If these roots are compromised, the tree fails to thrive and eventually dies. Roots are its lifeline.

Unhealthy roots produce weakness in human beings, too. For example, there was a time when cigarettes and smoking seemed stylish and sophisticated. The tobacco industry did its best to promote that image, especially through advertisement and celebrities. Teens are convinced to take up smoking to identify with their heroes, be accepted by their peer group, and look grown-up. For a relatively small price (not really), you can be as amazing as the people in the pictures.

But soon addiction takes hold. Smoking becomes dirty, expensive, and very unhealthy. You smell bad, and many folks no longer want to be around you. The seeds of attraction planted earlier in life seemed like a good idea, but their roots are rotten. The fruit is sickness and possibly an early death. Many fleshly attractions can result in the same bad fruit.

The Scriptures teach us about both good and bad fruit.

You, my brothers and sisters, were called to be free. But do not use your freedom to indulge the flesh; rather, serve one another humbly in love. For the entire law is fulfilled in keeping this one command: "Love your neighbor as yourself." If you bite and devour each other, watch out or you will be destroyed by each other.

So I say, walk by the Spirit, and you will not gratify the desires of the flesh. For the flesh desires what is contrary to the Spirit, and the Spirit what is contrary to the flesh. They are in conflict with each other, so that you are not to do whatever you want. But if you are led by the Spirit, you are not under the law.

—Galatians 5:13–18

Fruit of the Spirit

But the fruit of the Spirit is love, joy, peace, forbearance, kindness, goodness, faithfulness, gentleness and self-control. Against such things there is no law.

—Galatians 5:22–23

Do you feel a sense of longing when you read this list? Don't we all want to act like that? No one is there yet. However, the investment in such attributes of the Spirit is rewarding, both in your generation and for generations to come.

God is invested in you. He wants you to look like His Son. The Holy Spirit will help you. If you see something fleshly in your life that you can't overcome, ask Him. He will work in the circumstances of your life to bring about change. The fruit of the Spirit is produced when you walk with, submit to, and trust in Him.

Some people think that dressing modestly is a fruit of the Spirit or that being very serious shows strong roots. Some people think that if you speak about high-minded

Christian ideals, pray eloquently, or quote Scripture better than others, you must be walking with God. But these things are only surface factors. You need roots that grow deep and will endure in every season.

If you are a true believer with strong roots, you will make good decisions when no one is watching. You will spend time in the Word and pray. You will fall on your knees and worship God, whether you feel like it or not. This will keep you spiritually minded and connected with God at all times. You will provide your spirit with the nutrients and moisture it needs for growing good fruit.

The fruit of the Spirit comes from living in unity with God. When you do, good fruit grows naturally. The corruption of the flesh cannot live in the presence of the Holy Spirit. The flesh will diminish. The Spirit will grow stronger.

The fruits of the Spirit are so important, but many believers neglect them and fail to live them out consciously. As we discuss each fruit, keep asking yourself, "Do I practice this attribute? Do I strive for this characteristic? Am I making it a priority in my life?"

Love One Another

The first fruit of the Spirit mentioned in Galatians is love. Love (*agape*) is one of the most frequently used words in Paul's vocabulary, with variations of the word appearing over one hundred times in his writings.[5] It is significant that this is the fruit used to head up the nine graces of a Christian life found in Galatians.

Love seems to be a connecting point for the other fruit in Paul's list. To borrow the words of Caroline Leaf from *The Gift in You*, "Love and fear are the root emotions, and all other emotions grow from these. For example, out of love flow joy, peace, happiness, patience, kindness, gentleness, faithfulness, self-control, compassion, calmness, inspiration, excitement, hope, anticipation, and satisfaction."[6] It is quite difficult to practice the other fruit of the Spirit without first practicing love.

Oh, how this world needs romance! But this isn't the love Paul spoke of in 1 Corinthians. Romance may fade when the honeymoon is over, but godly love is designed to last a lifetime.

> *If I speak in the tongues of men or of angels, but do not have love, I am only a resounding gong or a clanging cymbal. If I have the gift of prophecy and can fathom all mysteries and all knowledge, and if I have a faith that can move mountains, but do not have love, I am nothing. If I give all I possess to the poor and give over my body to hardship that I may boast, but do not have love, I gain nothing.*
>
> *Love is patient, love is kind. It does not envy, it does not boast, it is not proud. It does not dishonor others, it is not self-seeking, it is not easily angered, it keeps no record of wrongs. Love does not delight in evil but rejoices with the truth. It always protects, always trusts, always hopes, always perseveres.*
>
> **—1 Corinthians 13:1–7**

This love doesn't consist of falling for a cute girl or swooning when a handsome guy talks to you. This is a deep, sacrificial kind of love. This love calls you to lay down your life for your brother (John 15:13). It's the kind that forgives time and time again (Matthew 18:21–22). This love brings out the best in everyone.

If you bring a drink to someone and that person doesn't notice the trouble you went through, this love doesn't get miffed. You only want to serve the person who thirsts. Do you have the kind of love that asks for nothing in return, or do you look for recognition?

Find Joy in Living

God takes joy in your joy—when you see the beauty of His creation, listen to the birds sing, enjoy the warmth of the spring sun on your skin, or watch your toddler play in the snow. Joy doesn't come from outside sources. It doesn't come from a raise at work or a kind word about your appearance. Joy exceeds happiness, bringing an unexplainable bliss that comes only from God. It explains how Christians can walk around with smiles on their faces even when trouble surrounds them. Despite day-to-day events affecting believers' emotions, their closeness to God allows them to experience the joy of life no matter the circumstances (Philippians 4:11–13).

Do you find that you have joy even when things are going badly, or are you constantly looking for something to cheer you up?

Embrace God's Peace

Peace is calm when there is a swirl of chaos around you. Who controls events? You? There's not much you can do, but if you and God are close, peace will be a by-product of your life.

> *The Lord is near. Do not be anxious about anything, but in every situation, by prayer and petition, with thanksgiving, present your requests to God. And the peace of God, which transcends all understanding, will guard your hearts and your minds in Christ Jesus.*
> **—Philippians 4:5b–7**

Share this peace with others around you. It is a fruit not easily found and desperately needed in today's world. Even if people mock you, your witness will remain in their minds and draw them to salvation.

Peace can reign in moments when it seems unnatural or doesn't seem to make sense. It's like living in the eye of the storm—chaos all around, hurricane winds on every side, but stillness in the middle of it all. It is possible to have that peace in spite of what's going on around you. You can experience peace beyond human understanding, just like Philippians 4:7 says. The key is to focus on the Lord rather than on the storm.

As mentioned in chapter 1, after I gave God my petitions through praise and worship (thanksgiving), peace came over me. Logically, I should have been panicking. It would have made sense to panic; it would have been understandable. But the peace of God defies logic, and my heart and mind were guarded from stress and anxiety.

Walk in Patience

Patience is a virtue. Everyone likes to say this because patience is so difficult to acquire! Another old saying is "God, give me patience—and give it to me now!"

This is an area that has always been difficult for me to practice. I'm a punctual person and hate being late to things, but my family (with four children) hasn't always shared this same conviction. Through the years, I have had to practice patience in the times we were running late. I haven't arrived yet, but I am sure that my family will continue to bless me with opportunities to grow in patience.

Patience is tough in the face of the harassment and assaults of daily life. Although it is trendy to blame our frenetic culture and fast pace for our impatience, it has been a problem from the beginning of time, and it usually leads to sin. It causes us to react to our current circumstances rather than trusting God and waiting for His timing.

Remember what happened when the Israelites got tired

of waiting for Moses to come down off the mountain? In their impatience, they built the golden calf (Exodus 32:1– 6). How about Esau, who could not wait to make his own lunch and sold his birthright for a bowl of soup (Genesis 25:29–34)? Perhaps the causes of our irritability have changed through time, but the root still lies in our flesh. God wants that to change.

Think about your reactions to people and the things that bother you. Do you weather the storms, or do you lash out, out-bullying the bully? The temptation is strong. That is why patience is a quality of God, not natural to the human ego. Yes, you need to pray for patience. And no, you can't have it right now, but it will come.

Practice Kindness

When God's goodness fills you, it overflows like water pouring from a cup (Luke 6:38). That's a picture of kindness. It doesn't cost you anything because it comes from God. The amazing thing about kindness is that it multiplies. When you are kind to others, others are kind to you, and you are doubly blessed. Proverbs 11:17 says, "Those who are kind benefit themselves, but the cruel bring ruin on themselves."

Don't worry about your own needs. They will be met in the process.

So do not worry, saying, "What shall we eat?" or "What shall we drink?" or "What shall we wear?" For the pagans run after all these things, and your heavenly Father knows that you need them. But seek first his kingdom and his righteousness, and all these things will be given to you as well.
—***Matthew 6:31–33***

Are you focused on your own needs and desires, or are you serving others when the cup of God's goodness overflows in your life? Serving others and working to meet their needs is central to the kindness that He desires us to demonstrate.

The Bible also says that a kind, gentle word "turns away wrath" (Proverbs 15:1). It is truly amazing to experience this first-hand when someone is berating you or speaking harshly. If you reply with kindness, it blows the other person away. It's not an easy thing to do, but the results are almost comical. Choosing to practice this fruit of the Spirit instead of reacting to anger with anger will always have a better outcome. God's kindness leads us to repentance (Romans 2:4), so it very well may happen that we could lead those around us to repentance by responding to their anger with kindness.

Choose Goodness

The LORD is righteous in all his ways and faithful in all he does. The LORD is near to all who call on him, to all who call on him in truth. He fulfills the desires of those who fear him; he hears their cry and saves them. The LORD watches over all who love him, but all the wicked he will destroy.

My mouth will speak in praise of the LORD. Let every creature praise his holy name for ever and ever.
—Psalm 145:17–21

We may be tempted to think about goodness in the context of God patting us on the head and reminding us to be good little boys and girls, but it speaks more to being gracious to those around us. It is about giving of ourselves to other people and not expecting anything in return.

Sometimes it is hard to wrap our minds around how good God is. David listed many ways in which He is good in the psalm above, but His attributes are truly endless. God is perfect. Perfection was lost with the fall of man, restored only in the life of Jesus. Nevertheless, a true believer longs to reflect that perfection. God's holiness drives away evil. When you commune with Him, you resist your flesh and are filled with the Spirit. Prefer right over wrong. Choose the goodness of God over Satan's evil every day. The Spirit will always show you the difference.

Be Faithful

Being in ministry for so long, I have come to appreciate faithfulness, but we must remember that our faithfulness must first be to the Lord. If your faithfulness is rooted in ministry, it may be appreciated by your pastor or leader, but it will eventually become unbalanced.

Faithfulness requires being trustworthy and reliable. God has called us to be solid in every area of our lives, including our relationships, our work, and our ministry. For those called as leaders to other believers, this is crucial.

When you are trustworthy, you hold the confidence of those around you. You follow through on your decisions, allowing the Spirit to guide you in wisdom. When you tell someone that you're going to do something, you do it. Nehemiah is a prime example of this kind of stick-to-it-iveness.

When Nehemiah heard that the walls of Jerusalem had been destroyed during the years of Judah's exile, he wept and prayed for God's favor to repair them (Nehemiah 1). Nehemiah persisted in the face of great opposition and spiritual warfare, and he inspired others to stick with him until the job was done. Nehemiah was faithful to God, and God was faithful to him.

The time for rebuilding the city walls has passed, but

the Lord still has countless tasks to be done in building up
His kingdom on earth. Your own assignment may seem
insignificant to you, but there is a promise inherent in doing it well. The issue is faithfulness, not the perceived
importance of the job.

I remember when the San Francisco Giants were in the
World Series a few years ago. I have been a Giants fan
since I was a little boy, and this was exciting. But I had
volunteered to teach an eight-week community class.
There were supposed to be a ton of people participating in
this class, but only a handful would show up to the classes.
Every night our class met, there was a World Series or a
playoff game on, and it was killing me. I really wanted to
watch the game, but I had committed to teach the class,
even if only two people showed up. I followed through
with my commitment because I was practicing faithfulness.

> *Whoever can be trusted with very little can also be trusted
> with much, and whoever is dishonest with very little will
> also be dishonest with much.*
> **—Luke 16:10**

> *Who then is the faithful and wise servant, whom the mas-
> ter has put in charge of the servants in his household to
> give them their food at the proper time? It will be good for
> that servant whose master finds him doing so when he re-
> turns. Truly I tell you, he will put him in charge of all his
> possessions.*
> **—Matthew 24:45–47**

Are you reliable? Can others depend on you to do your
part? What if the Lord returns? Will your lamp be full
(Matthew 25:1–13)? Will you be busy at your assignment
for the Kingdom? It is pretty straightforward.

At that time the kingdom of heaven will be like ten virgins who took their lamps and went out to meet the bridegroom. Five of them were foolish and five were wise. The foolish ones took their lamps but did not take any oil with them. The wise ones, however, took oil in jars along with their lamps. The bridegroom was a long time in coming, and they all became drowsy and fell asleep.
                                              —Matthew 25:1–5

Be Gentle

Come to me, all you who are weary and burdened, and I will give you rest. Take my yoke upon you and learn from me, for I am gentle and humble in heart, and you will find rest for your souls.
                                              —Matthew 11:28–29

Gentleness isn't a weakness, but a strength. Gentleness brings peace to the broken-hearted and refreshes those who struggle to keep their heads above water. Another word we could use here is *humility*. This fruit of the Spirit requires us to be submissive and to demonstrate a teachable spirit.

Gentleness is rare in our get-over-it and man-up culture. Some people falsely assume that if you don't act aggressively when dealing with others, then you are weak. That is very far from the truth. Gentleness disarms people who want to oppose you or find fault with your message, as Paul told Timothy:

And the Lord's servant must not be quarrelsome but must be kind to everyone, able to teach, not resentful. Opponents must be gently instructed, in the hope that God will grant them repentance leading them to a knowledge of the truth,

and that they will come to their senses and escape from the
trap of the devil, who has taken them captive to do his will.
—*2 Timothy 2:24–26*

I am not saying that we should practice self-deprecia-
tion or let other people walk all over us. But if the attitude
in our hearts is to dominate other people, then we are not
practicing the fruit of the Spirit. When you walk into a
room, are you loud and forceful, or do you fill the room
with the gentle grace of God's love?

Develop Self-Control

The fight between the flesh and the spirit is a constant
battle of right and wrong. Self-control is vital to overcoming your worldly desires. Paul put it simply: run like you
mean it.

I think that most people struggle with self-control. This
is why there are so many self-help groups today. These
groups have their place, but there are so many people
struggling with their urges regarding food, money, sleep,
or other self-gratifying desires. Some of these are even
natural desires that have been misplaced.

However, self-control is absolutely necessary to grow
as a believer. It takes discipline to be a disciple. It doesn't
seem like much for us to practice self-sacrifice in our lives
when Jesus gave Himself up to death.

We will spend a lifetime learning to deny ourselves,
pick up our crosses, and follow Him (Matthew 16:24).
This starts with denying ourselves and practicing self-control. One of the most effective ways to do this is through
fasting. By denying our flesh, we learn how to control our
actions.

Therefore I do not run like someone running aimlessly; I do not fight like a boxer beating the air. No, I strike a blow to my body and make it my slave so that after I have preached to others, I myself will not be disqualified for the prize.
—1 Corinthians 9:26–27

And when someone else wants to punch you out:

Do not repay anyone evil for evil. Be careful to do what is right in the eyes of everyone. If it is possible, as far as it depends on you, live at peace with everyone. Do not take revenge, my dear friends, but leave room for God's wrath, for it is written: "It is mine to avenge; I will repay," says the Lord.
—Romans 12:17–19

Finally, Peter covered all the bases:

Dear friends, I urge you, as foreigners and exiles, to abstain from sinful desires, which wage war against your soul. Live such good lives among the pagans that, though they accuse you of doing wrong, they may see your good deeds and glorify God on the day he visits us.
—1 Peter 2:11–12

Do you always do what Jesus would do? If you examine yourself honestly, you may feel devastated by the weakness you see. That is not uncommon, but don't stop here. Go quickly to the next chapter. There is hope, and it is within reach. Keep reading!

WORKBOOK

Chapter Three Questions

Question: What are some difficulties that people may blame God for or get angry at God about that are the natural consequences of poor choices? What are some demands that you or others have of God? Are these expectations based on the promises of Scripture or on selfishness?

_____

_____

_____

_____

_____

_____

_____

_____

_____

_____

Question: What is the difference between outward tokens of godliness and true fruit of the Spirit? How do you know if you are growing these fruits?

_____

_____

_____

_____

_____

_____

_____

_____

_____

_____

Question: Look at the list and descriptions of the fruit of the Spirit. Which of these is most challenging for you? Why? What steps can you take to cultivate this fruit more intentionally?

_____

_____

_____

_____

_____

_____

_____

_____

_____

_____

_____

Action: Memorize Galatians 5:22–23. Do a study on each of these qualities in Scripture. What does it mean, and how is it exemplified?

Chapter Three Notes

_____

_____

_____

_____

_____

_____

_____

_____

_____

_____

_____

_____

_____

_____

_____

_____

_____

_____

_____

_____

_____

_____

CHAPTER FOUR

Avoid the Lusts of the Flesh

The acts of the flesh are obvious: sexual immorality, impurity and debauchery; idolatry and witchcraft; hatred, discord, jealousy, fits of rage, selfish ambition, dissensions, factions and envy; drunkenness, orgies, and the like. I warn you, as I did before, that those who live like this will not inherit the kingdom of God.
—Galatians 5:19–21

Paul said that the acts of the flesh are obvious, and he listed them for us in Galatians.

Sexual immorality and impurity involve sexual relations outside of marriage, including premarital sex, pornography, erotic literature, and the list goes on. If you can't bring it before your parents or you can't tell your spouse what you're doing, is it right? No.

Idolatry and witchcraft involve worshipping anything other than God, practicing a perverted religion. This can include the worship of your car, sports, a celebrity, or even your emotions, good or bad, such as self-esteem. God is jealous, and He would have you worship Him and Him alone (Exodus 34:14).

Discord means living without harmony, such as starting fights, gossiping, or finding ways to split families and friends.

Jealousy and fits of rage are also sinful. Part of walking in the Spirit must be self-control. If you're a hothead, ask God to help you control your temper.

Selfish ambition, dissension, and factions all stem from the same selfish desires. Being a conniving person and deceiving others to get what you want is wrong. Causing fights between others and creating factions to war, all for your own glory, is wrong. Claiming to do it for His glory is just as wrong and misguided.

Envy means wanting what someone else has. Don't covet other people's belongings, such as their cars, spouses, jobs, kids, or even their dogs. Just enjoy what God has given to you. Giving thanks for what you have will help you to avoid envy.

Drunkenness, orgies, and the like must be avoided. If you lose control of your mind because of medicine, alcohol, drugs, or any other self-induced reason, you have opened yourself up to sin and its consequences.

Jesus' redeeming work on the cross has set you free from condemnation. The gift and inner workings of the Holy Spirit tell you the way you should go. Your flesh only holds you down and keeps you focused on things that fail to satisfy your soul and keep you from growing in love. The flesh is selfish and demanding. It clamors for attention and whines when it is ignored. You need to recognize the voice of your flesh and shut it down.

I remember times in college when I would be walking toward the cafeteria, ravenous, but would make the decision to turn back and pray. Why? Because I wanted to let my flesh know that it was under the subjection of the Holy Spirit. It wasn't easy, by any means, but it was an extremely effective way to learn to crucify the flesh.

Why sow seeds that cause you to obsess over finances,

bitterness, sex, or idols like your vanity and a consuming need for more and more things? The flesh and the Spirit work against each other. If you're doing things to feed the flesh, gratifying your physical senses, you're in direct opposition to the Spirit.

Like oil and water, today's Republicans and Democrats, and Raider and 49er fans, the flesh and the Spirit don't mix. The two cannot inhabit one body. You must choose the one you will follow.

In the book of Joshua, when he was a very old man and ready to die, Joshua gathered the leaders of Israel together and blessed them. He had led them through many difficult years of battle. They had defeated their enemies and settled in the land that God had given them. Now it was time to go to their homes and just live their lives. Joshua posed one final choice for them to consider for their future as a nation:

> *Now fear the LORD and serve him with all faithfulness. Throw away the gods your ancestors worshiped beyond the Euphrates River and in Egypt, and serve the LORD. But if serving the LORD seems undesirable to you, then choose for yourselves this day whom you will serve, whether the gods your ancestors served beyond the Euphrates, or the gods of the Amorites, in whose land you are living. But as for me and my household, we will serve the LORD.*
> *—Joshua 24:14–15*

We need to be all-in believers. The day for wishy-washy Christianity is over. If you don't serve God, then you serve the devil and your flesh. It needs to be normal to live radically for Christ rather than any other way. To live this radical lifestyle in today's culture, we have to put away the things of the flesh and walk in the Spirit.

At times, you may be able to pretend that you have it all together. But oh, how quickly that house built on sand crumbles. Building on the Rock of Christ is the only answer, but how do you do that?

> *Therefore everyone who hears these words of mine and puts them into practice is like a wise man who built his house on the rock. The rain came down, the streams rose, and the winds blew and beat against that house; yet it did not fall, because it had its foundation on the rock. But everyone who hears these words of mine and does not put them into practice is like a foolish man who built his house on sand. The rain came down, the streams rose, and the winds blew and beat against that house, and it fell with a great crash.*
> **—Matthew 7:24–27**

Intentional Obedience

Planting bad seeds grows weak roots that produce terrible fruit. But worship, prayer, and reading God's Word produce strong roots and godly fruit. It is impossible for fruit like grapes to grow when it is disconnected from the vine. Jesus called Himself "the true vine" (John 15:1), the source of our fruit. In order to sustain healthy fruit, we must be united to Him and abide with Him (John 15:1–8).

Any fruit produced apart from the vine is useless to us because it has been tainted by our sinful nature. Each of us was born with a sinful nature, but Christ came so that in dying to our old nature, we could live united with Him (Romans 5:12–6:23). But we must make a choice each day to put our flesh to death and walk in the life He has given us.

There is a maxim about a goldfish swimming in a fishbowl. It looks longingly at the world and wants to walk around outside of the fishbowl. With only one small jump, the fish leaves the safety of the bowl and its confinement. But the air outside is unfit to breathe. Too late, the fish recognizes its mistake in following its whim. As it is gasping its last, someone finds it, lifts it up, and drops its oxygen-starved body back into the water. It took a few minutes to revive, but someone wiser than the fish saved it from the fatal consequence of its poor choice. Does this sound vaguely familiar? God designed you to live in a fishbowl, too. The bowl is made up of His ordinances for holy living. These guidelines are the perfect environment for health and well-being. If you feel confined, you may not understand or appreciate the life-giving benefits of the boundaries God put in place. You may also be surprised to learn that biblical principles are rooted in love.

When a Pharisee asked Jesus what the greatest commandment was, Jesus answered:

"Love the Lord your God with all your heart and with all your soul and with all your mind." This is the first and greatest commandment. And the second is like it: "Love your neighbor as yourself." All the Law and the Prophets hang on these two commandments.
—Matthew 22:37–40

Living in disobedience can lead to disaster. Obedience to God's commands produces a blessed and fulfilled life. His commands are directives intended to make love your highest aim. Choosing to love God over feeding your own desires delivers you from the enemies around and within you. Let the Lord look after your interests. He can do a much better job than you ever could anyway. The ravages of this world will not overtake you. Jesus promised:

In this world you will have trouble. But take heart! I have overcome the world.
—John 16:33b

Walking in the Spirit Is a Process

I will put my laws in their minds and write them on their hearts. I will be their God, and they will be my people.
—Hebrews 8:10b

Waking up one day and deciding to let the Spirit take control of your life may change your heart instantly, but the battle with your flesh is ongoing. Becoming like Christ is less like a microwave experience and more like a slow-cooker process. I have never been a professional athlete, a dancer, or a musician, but I understand that they all have one thing in common: muscle memory. If you do something over and over and over in the exact same way, eventually your body strings together a long series of movements and completes them without much thought on your part. That is what gives the rest of us the pleasure of watching a triple axel or an Argentine tango or listening to a Brahms concerto.

It is much the same with learning to overcome your flesh and love others like Jesus did. At first, it may seem awkward and forced, but after doing the same thing over and over, it becomes second nature. Maybe it's not easy, but it's certainly not impossible.

For this very reason, make every effort to add to your faith goodness; and to goodness, knowledge; and to knowledge, self-control; and to self-control, perseverance; and to perseverance, godliness; and to godliness, mutual affection; and to mutual affection, love. For if you possess these qualities in increasing measure, they will keep you from being ineffective and unproductive in your knowledge of our Lord Jesus Christ.
—2 Peter 1:5–8

NOT OF THIS WORLD · 65

Notice that Peter said, "For if you possess these qualities in increasing measure...." There is grace in this
statement. God isn't calling you to be perfect immediately. You're going to fail, but He will forgive you as you
stay connected with Him (1 John 1:9). God is calling you
to be more loving, more joyful, more peace-filled, more
forbearing, more kind, more faithful, gentler, and more
self-controlled than you were yesterday. And if you're following Him, you will be. Your flesh will be overcome by
the Spirit at work in you.

The world will never help you to overcome the flesh.
If you step on someone's toes, the world will say, "He had
it coming." They will tell you that gentleness is weakness,
that forbearance allows people to take advantage of you,
and that kindness is naivete in this dog-eat-dog world.
"Look out for Number One," they will say. But you are no
longer of this world. Just tell them that you've moved on.

> But you are a chosen people, a royal priesthood, a holy na-
> tion, God's special possession, that you may declare the
> praises of him who called you out of darkness into his won-
> derful light. Once you were not a people, but now you are
> the people of God; once you had not received mercy, but
> now you have received mercy.
> **—1 Peter 2:9–10**

I have more to tell you about these people, your new
home, the church. Perhaps you think that there couldn't
be much new to say about the church. After all, the church
has been around your whole life. But Paul invested his life
in the first-century body of Christ. His letters to the
churches he had planted and nurtured reveal his love and
care for them. He worked to keep them safe from false

doctrines, to settle disputes, and to teach spiritual principles. He also *liked* these people. Let's move on to the next chapter now and see what he had to say.

WORKBOOK

Chapter Four Questions

Question: Give some examples of the acts of the flesh. Which of these do you find most tempting? How can you walk in your freedom in Christ instead of in slavery to sin?

_____

_____

_____

_____

_____

_____

_____

_____

_____

_____

_____

Question: What is the world's view of obedience? How does obedience to God create a joyous life?

_____

_____

_____

_____

_____

_____

_____

_____

_____

_____

_____

Question: How is choosing obedience like being an athlete or a musician? How should you respond when you mess up? How does God respond?

_____

_____

_____

_____

_____

_____

_____

_____

_____

_____

_____

_____

Action: For each fruit, Satan has a cheap substitute (sex and fleeting romance instead of biblical love, pleasure instead of joy, etc.). Finish the list of substitutes. Compare and contrast what Satan and the world offer versus what Christ offers. How can producing the fruit of the Spirit lead others to Jesus?

Chapter Four Notes

_____

_____

_____

_____

_____

_____

_____

_____

_____

_____

_____

_____

_____

_____

_____

_____

_____

_____

_____

CHAPTER FIVE

Fellowship with Others

Consequently, you are no longer foreigners and strangers, but fellow citizens with God's people and also members of his household, built on the foundation of the apostles and prophets, with Christ Jesus himself as the chief cornerstone. In him the whole building is joined together and rises to become a holy temple in the Lord. And in him you too are being built together to become a dwelling in which God lives by his Spirit.
—Ephesians 2:19–22

The church was God's idea, and He gave it life. The church is not just an institution that demands our time and money to maintain its own existence, and the church is not a building. Scripture calls the church the bride of Christ (Ephesians 5:22–32), "the body of Christ" (Ephesians 4:12), and "the people of God" (1 Peter 2:10).

Why is the church so important? We need each other for strength, for accountability, for protection, for comfort, and for shared joy. Human beings aren't meant to be alone. No person is an island. If you live without fellowship, you may be lonely and depressed, rather than enjoying a much richer life as a child of God. Let me share a short story to demonstrate my point.

There's More to Church Than Bible Study

Bob groaned as he rolled over in bed. He stretched and watched his wife walk over from the closet.

"Are you coming to church today?" she asked, putting on an earring. "The kids and I would love to spend time with you."

"Not today. It was a long week."

"You haven't been to church in several months." She slipped on a heel.

He pulled a pillow over his head. "I know. It's just that church isn't really for me. And you know how insane work has been. Today is my only day off."

"All right, Bob. Maybe next week."

Bob couldn't avoid hearing the disappointment in her voice as he set aside the pillow and watched her leave the room.

Bob was exhausted, and the last thing he needed was people greeting him, asking how things were, and—oh, all those things that people did at church. He couldn't give up two hours today.

His wife popped her head back through the bedroom door one last time. "We're going to lunch with Chris and Marley after the service. Want me to pick you up something to eat?"

"Nah, I'm okay. Have fun. Next week I'll be up to going."

Bob felt sorry for Chris, who seemed to love going to church. He could not see the appeal.

Bob sat on the couch, watching football for a while, a soda in one hand and a snack in the other. He checked his watch. *Shouldn't they be finishing up with lunch soon?* A ring on the doorbell pulled Bob out of the game and off the couch.

Police.

His wife had been riding with Marley, while Chris was

driving all the kids in the car behind them. The wives had been hit head-on by another car, and both women had been killed instantly.

The remote slipped from his fingers, just before Bob dropped to the floor.

Over the next weeks, Bob struggled with his loss, but he found no one who could help. Chris was the only person who reached out, and the two grew closer through their mutual grief.

Bob was lonely and despairing as he saw Chris's church family rally around Chris in his time of need. Although the same people had tried to help Bob and his kids by bringing food, they just weren't close enough to Bob to know what he really needed. Bob had no close friends in whom he could confide, no one to help bear his burdens.

Thinking that it might not be too late to attend services, Bob joined Chris at the men's breakfast. But the support and camaraderie Chris received from the other men made Bob uncomfortable and even a little jealous.

He realized that he should have been in church with his wife when he had the chance. Although he started attending after she died, the deep fellowship he so desperately needed had not had enough time to develop. He was tempted to blame God for his isolation, but a few people reached out and wouldn't let go of him. Slowly, over time, Bob began to see that God is good and that Christ's love within the church is more than lip service.

More than just assuaging our feelings, being part of a church family has profound long-term effects. I've watched most families who make church attendance a priority stay together. Their closeness is touching. The children are healthy, both spiritually and emotionally, and they have friends who share their values. When life gets hard—with the tragedy of a lost loved one, the destruction of a house or vehicle through fire or an accident, or the loss of a job—the church rallies around the broken family.

Excuses for not attending church are as varied as an individual's conscience:

> *The Bible is vague on whether I need to go to church.*
>
> *The church is full of hypocrites.*
>
> *I prefer meeting with God in the mountains.*
>
> *No one will care if I miss one Sunday. The game is going to be so amazing!*
>
> *Our children come first, and they have an event during that time.*

It is hard to dismiss the Scripture passages that require believers to assemble. There's an integral shift in your life when you are attending church consistently. You are stating that God is a priority in your life. Could golf really be more important than God? Fellowship with other believers gets your focus off yourself and onto God and the mission He has given to His people.

> *And let us consider how we may spur one another on toward love and good deeds, not giving up meeting together, as some are in the habit of doing, but encouraging one another—and all the more as you see the Day approaching.*
> *—Hebrews 10:24–25*

After Jesus rose from the dead and ascended into heaven, His disciples instinctively gathered together to share their profound experiences and make plans to move forward with His command to make disciples of all nations. Believers weren't on their own. This was intentional because God designed us to live in fellowship with each other. Even Jesus lived in community with His family and disciples.

We see this longing for community all across America. It may seem silly, but things like CrossFit prove this. Individuals don't join a CrossFit gym just because they want to better themselves physically. They could do that on their own. People gravitate to the community aspect of this health and fitness movement.

> *They all joined together constantly in prayer, along with the women and Mary the mother of Jesus, and with his brothers.*
>
> **—Acts 1:14**

And who could ever discount the day of Pentecost, when they all received the power to accomplish the mission?

> *When the day of Pentecost came, they were all together in one place. Suddenly a sound like the blowing of a violent wind came from heaven and filled the whole house where they were sitting. They saw what seemed to be tongues of fire that separated and came to rest on each of them. All of them were filled with the Holy Spirit and began to speak in other tongues as the Spirit enabled them.*
>
> **—Acts 2:1–4**

Note that "they were all together in one place," praying. That sounds like a church service to me.

The Church's Mission

> *Then Jesus came to them and said, "All authority in heaven and on earth has been given to me. Therefore go and make disciples of all nations, baptizing them in the name of the*

Father and of the Son and of the Holy Spirit, and teaching them to obey everything I have commanded you. And surely I am with you always, to the very end of the age."
                                        —Matthew 28:18–20

We are to proclaim to the world who God is, that we are sinners, and that Jesus died for our sins and rose again. As Romans 10:9 says, "If you declare with your mouth, 'Jesus is Lord,' and believe in your heart that God raised him from the dead, you will be saved." But that's not the end of it.

Look at the first several chapters of Acts, when people were added to the church. What happened next? Christians shared everything so completely that people wanted to be together (Acts 2:42–47).

...being confident of this, that he who began a good work in you will carry it on to completion until the day of Christ Jesus.
                                        —Philippians 1:6

Over and over again, Paul talked about Christians who came together for meetings. Paul approached the subject as if church attendance wasn't even questioned. Attendance was never an *if*; it was a *when*. All were expected to participate.

What then shall we say, brothers and sisters? When you come together, each of you has a hymn, or a word of instruction, a revelation, a tongue or an interpretation. Everything must be done so that the church may be built up.
                                        —1 Corinthians 14:26

Almost all of Paul's epistles in the New Testament were written to churches, rather than individuals, with the exceptions of 1 and 2 Timothy, Titus, and Philemon. The length and detail of his letters show how much Paul cared about the welfare of these church plants. He carefully nurtured them as part of God's plan in order to keep the believers on track and caring for one another.

Missing Isn't an Option

God created you to need other Christians, but when you're not right with God, when you're not communing with Him, fellowship with other believers is usually the first thing to go. Unfortunately, when you cut the power cord from the church, you lose your strength and connection to the vital Source: God.

Fellowship doesn't mean just showing up Sunday morning to a big building. Join a small group that meets regularly to pray and encourage each other. Also, you may want to find an accountability partner, someone you trust who will keep an eye on you, ask the hard questions, and look out for your best interests.

Gathering together with other Christians on Sunday prepares you for the week. Many believers say, "If I miss one Sunday gathering, I'm lost. It's as if my battery isn't charged, and by the middle of the week, my energy is gone." I've heard this time and again. Why miss out on this kind of energy by staying home and watching television? Why miss out on godly encouragement just to hit a ball around on a field of grass? Why miss out on the comfort you could receive to stay home and wallow in your pain? Think about it. A true believer attends church.

Once we agree that church is important to God and to our lives, what about widening the tent pegs? In the words of Isaiah, "Enlarge the place of your tent, stretch your tent curtains wide, do not hold back; lengthen your cords, strengthen your stakes" (Isaiah 54:2). It's time to consider how to welcome others into the body of Christ.

In the next chapter, we will explore ways to share our commitment and excitement and bring others to salvation and life in Christ. Evangelism is not as hard as you may think! In fact, it will likely bless you as much as it blesses those who respond to God's call.

NOT OF THIS WORLD · 79

WORKBOOK

Chapter Five Questions

Question: Why is the current cultural sentiment of "I love Jesus; I just don't like the church" both unbiblical and harmful? How would you respond to someone who expresses that idea?

_____

_____

_____

_____

_____

_____

_____

_____

_____

_____

_____

Question: What are reasons a Christian might skip or abandon church? What are some blessings that come through being connected to and involved in a local church that cannot be obtained by just watching church online?

_____

_____

_____

_____

_____

_____

_____

_____

_____

_____

_____

Question: How is the early church described in the New Testament? How can modern believers follow this model?

_____

_____

_____

_____

_____

_____

_____

_____

_____

_____

_____

Action: If your church has a class for new members, find out when the next session is and make plans to attend. If you have already been through the class, ask your pastor if you can attend again for the purpose of encouraging and building friendships with those who are new to your church. If your church does not have a class for new members, plan a time when you can talk with your spiritual leader about facilitating a new-believers fellowship.

Chapter Five Notes

_____

_____

_____

_____

_____

_____

_____

_____

_____

_____

_____

_____

_____

_____

_____

_____

_____

_____

_____

_____

CHAPTER SIX

Share Your Faith

Then Jesus came to them and said, "All authority in heaven and on earth has been given to me. Therefore go and make disciples of all nations, baptizing them in the name of the Father and of the Son and of the Holy Spirit, and teaching them to obey everything I have commanded you. And surely I am with you always, to the very end of the age."
—Matthew 28:18–20

Not all people come to Christ in a spectacular way. Some have stories of drugs and hitting a wall to the point that their choice became either God or death. Some were rescued from a pit of unimaginable sin. You probably have heard this kind of beautiful and inspiring testimony. But few lives are that dramatic. Commonly, life is a daily rhythm of working, eating, sleeping, and spending time with family, with the occasional adventure.

Most of us don't feel the need to be rescued from some kind of trap we have built for ourselves. Rather, we tend to search for the meaning of life—typically in all the wrong places. We rarely consider ourselves sinful until God prepares our hearts to see or hear the true meaning of sin. Jesus said, "No one can come to me unless the Father

who sent me draws them, and I will raise them up at the
last day" (John 6:44).

Unless the Father Draws Them

How does the Father draw someone? Life struggles,
natural disasters, war, and poverty can bring people to
their knees as they recognize their need for God. A joyful
experience, such as the birth of a child, the deliverance of
a loved one, or the indescribable beauty of nature, can
cause someone to succumb to the goodness of God. The
Father can use supernatural things, too, such as dreams,
visions, near-death experiences, or undeniable encounters
with God Himself (just ask Paul). Some people have the
great fortune of simply believing the truth at a young age.

But more often than not, the Father uses Christians to
draw other people to Jesus. He invites us to participate in
the work and the joy of a sinner redeemed. Prayer is one
way to do this. As we pray fervently for our loved ones
and friends, God's power is unleashed in their lives. They
may never know that we are praying for them, but God
knows, and God hears. If it takes longer than we think it
should, we must keep praying. The Lord loves those people even more than we do, and He will never give up as
long as they have breath.

The Father also draws people to Jesus by the Spirit.
There is a common saying that is popular on the internet
these days: "Preach the gospel at all times. Use words if
necessary." Some people say that this is a quote from
Saint Francis; others argue that it's not. Either way, it
points out a significant truth. Actions are not more important than words, but you need both to be consistent and
win over hardened hearts and closed minds.

You may open someone's heart with a kind act or some
other comfort that you offer as you demonstrate the fruit
of the Spirit. This is God's love made tangible, water for

NOT OF THIS WORLD · 85

a thirsty soul. Perhaps you may grab their attention with the way you carry yourself or raise your children or speak to your spouse. You don't have to try to be super-spiritual. Just be yourself. The Father knows what each person is looking for.

Your life is on public display, and if you're close to Jesus, it will show, especially in trials. As you live your life before men as a testimony of Christ, remember that you don't need to sugarcoat the gospel, hide your struggles, or make people think that being a Christian is always fantastic and easy. Consider how God used the disciples' lives to change the history of the world.

The disciples did as Jesus told them to do in Mark 16:15: "Go into all the world and proclaim the gospel to the whole creation" (ESV). They followed those words to the letter, demonstrating the life of a believer by word and by deed. Signs and wonders followed them in all of their travels. But the world and the devil hated their success. Tradition tells us that most of the disciples closest to Jesus were brutally persecuted and martyred for their faith. Yet their martyrdom only proved the truth and power of the gospel. Not one of them recanted, not even in the face of death. What a testimony to those around them of their love for and fidelity to Christ!

Tent Meetings and Stadiums

A third way the Father draws people is by simple invitation. You can welcome people into the Kingdom by getting them to the right place at the right time. The key to Jesus' charge to evangelize has always been about relationship, before and after salvation.

Many ministries today offer opportunities to hear the gospel in a non-threatening yet powerful way. The appeal of this movement shows how hungry people really are. God will bring people to you who are ripe for hearing the gospel. Take them to revival meetings (yes, go with them!), where they can hear the gospel preached with clarity and power. Some people may be more open to finding someone who can explain more about God in private. Maybe the person they are looking for is *you*. It all starts with you caring enough to step out in faith and offer them life.

Billy Graham was one of the twentieth century's most influential preachers. He spoke all over the world and met with many world leaders. Under his preaching, hundreds of thousands made professions of faith in large public gatherings. Billy realized that any decision made at one of his crusades was not the end of the story. He said, "Being a Christian is more than just an instantaneous conversion; it is a daily process whereby you grow to be more and more like Christ."[7]

Discipleship

Jesus' instruction was to "make disciples of all nations, baptizing them in the name of the Father and of the Son and of the Holy Spirit, and teaching them to obey everything I have commanded you" (Matthew 28:19–20a).

Passing down what you've learned in the Christian life isn't just a good idea; it's a command to you from Jesus Himself. Do you have a family tradition that passes down from generation to generation? Maybe tips and key bits of wisdom are passed down, over and over, from mother and father to children. Discipleship works the same way. It is much like raising a child because it requires your involvement long after someone makes the initial decision to follow Christ.

How do you go about teaching new believers? One way is through a Bible study in which Scripture is read and discussed, especially passages that detail the Christian life and its challenges. You can explain to new believers the difficulties and joys of being a Christian, share your own experiences, and work through difficult passages together with them. This kind of care and guidance prevents false doctrines and false prophets from robbing new believers of their faith and their connection to the church. Don't forget that the devil does not want believers to grow up in Christ.

Why is so little of this being done? Perhaps because it's not showy. We love to say, "We had eight people accept Christ in our church today." But to say, "We made some progress in our walk with Christ," is less exciting.

Part of the problem is that discipleship is a long process that takes years, maybe a lifetime, and it is difficult to make that kind of commitment and put in that kind of time. Our transient culture hinders that level of commitment as well. However, even a short-term commitment understood up front is better than ignoring the need altogether.

Discipleship also requires transparency. As Paul wrote, "all have sinned and fall short of the glory of God" (Romans 3:23). He also said that "all are justified freely by his grace through the redemption that came by Christ Jesus" (Romans 3:24). Sharing your mistakes and sins in order to receive another's instruction makes you very vulnerable. It's hard to admit your failures, perhaps an addiction to pornography or alcohol. It's embarrassing to admit that you love gossip or that you struggle with pride. It requires the strength and humility only available through the Spirit. Be sure to pray regularly for His protection and guidance.

Small groups can help to share the responsibility of teaching a new believer. If one person has had issues with sin, he or she can help the others as the group grows in trust.

Accountability partners are another vital tool that is often overlooked. Why do we ask someone to go on a diet with us? The feeling that we are not alone helps us not to eat that donut we crave. The same is true with sin. Whether the struggle involves a bad temper, sexual infidelity, drugs, alcohol, or a host of other possibilities, a righteous, loving person watching out for you can be priceless. And the reward for your accountability partner is eternal.

Jesus gave His life so that *all* might be saved. His passion for the unsaved has never diminished. He wants to give you His heart for the lost and share with you the desire to bring them safely into the kingdom of heaven. Jesus' last words, the most important thing on His heart as He ascended to the Father, show that discipleship is His mission until the end of the world, and He wants it to be yours as well.

I want to discuss one final aspect of Christian living in the next chapter. When you add this element to worship, prayer, the fruit of the Spirit, overcoming the flesh, embracing the church, evangelism, and discipleship, you will have the recipe for living life to the fullest as a fervent believer!

WORKBOOK

Chapter Six Questions

Question: What are some of the ways God draws people to Himself? What is the importance of a believer's actions in drawing unsaved people to Christ?

_____

_____

_____

_____

_____

_____

_____

_____

_____

_____

_____

Question: How would you define *discipleship*? Do you think that most new believers are adequately discipled? Why or why not? Who discipled you? What are some tools that can be used for discipleship (e.g. Christian living books)?

_____

_____

_____

_____

_____

_____

_____

_____

_____

_____

Question: Do you feel equipped and prepared to share the gospel? Why or why not? What role does fear play in keeping people from sharing their faith? (Be specific!)

_____

_____

_____

_____

_____

_____

_____

_____

_____

_____

_____

_____

Question: How can believers learn to share their faith? How can they be trained to disciple others? What steps can you take to be better at evangelizing and discipling others?

_____

_____

_____

_____

_____

_____

_____

_____

_____

_____

Action: Share your testimony of how you came to Christ. (It may be helpful to outline with bullet points first.) Practice by sharing your testimony with a Christian friend or a small group. Then find a time to meet with an unsaved friend and share your story with him or her.

Chapter Six Notes

_____

_____

_____

_____

_____

_____

_____

_____

_____

_____

_____

_____

_____

_____

_____

_____

_____

_____

CHAPTER SEVEN

Give from the Heart

Jesus sat down opposite the place where the offerings were put and watched the crowd putting their money into the temple treasury. Many rich people threw in large amounts. But a poor widow came and put in two very small copper coins, worth only a few cents.

Calling his disciples to him, Jesus said, "Truly I tell you, this poor widow has put more into the treasury than all the others. They all gave out of their wealth; but she, out of her poverty, put in everything—all she had to live on."
—Mark 12:41–44

Jesus watched the people giving their money at the temple. Why? What was He looking for, and why was He so pleased with this particular widow? The money in the temple treasury paid for the services the temple provided. With all the money the rich threw in, this poor woman could have skipped her puny gift—if the actual cash value were the issue. No one would have even noticed her gift, but that was not the point. Proportionately, this widow put in more than all the rest, for she gave "all she had to live on."

Maybe she thought long and hard about where she

should spend her last coins, and she showed her love for God and her trust in Him by her choice. She chose to trust God completely to supply her needs. She put all of her coins in the box.

> *And my God will meet all your needs according to the riches of his glory in Christ Jesus.*
> **—Philippians 4:19**

If you are poor and find it hard to give to others and to God, you can ask for faith to believe deep within you that you will not sink if you obey His call. Have you learned enough about God's character to know that He will care for you? If not, keep worshipping Him and get to know Him better.

Rather than poverty, however, some people are driven by greed. Jesus taught about the futility of greed in one of His parables:

> Then he said to them, "Watch out! Be on your guard against all kinds of greed; life does not consist in an abundance of possessions."

> And he told them this parable: "The ground of a certain rich man yielded an abundant harvest. He thought to himself, 'What shall I do? I have no place to store my crops.'

> "Then he said, 'This is what I'll do. I will tear down my barns and build bigger ones, and there I will store my surplus grain. And I'll say to myself, "You have plenty of grain laid up for many years. Take life easy; eat, drink and be merry."'

> "But God said to him, 'You fool! This very night your life will be demanded from you. Then who will get what you have prepared for yourself?'

"This is how it will be with whoever stores up things for themselves but is not rich toward God."
—Luke 12:15-21

We all know that we can't take it with us when we die. Paradoxically, greed is a much greater temptation in a land of plenty than it is in a country where everyone is living on the edge. When your neighbor parks a new car in his driveway and you are driving last year's model (or worse), you feel a twinge inside of you. Right? Envy, pride, and an unreasonable sense of deprivation can overtake you in an instant.

This is the lust of the flesh undisguised. You can't take it with you, but somehow you still want to collect as much as you can, certainly more than your neighbor has. Blinders that keep you from seeing what your neighbors have won't really help, but the Spirit of God in your life will. He will help you to be thankful for what He has already given you and to store up treasure in heaven instead.

God doesn't need anything. He already owns everything. Giving is a heart issue, an attitude check. God loves you, and that's why you give: because you love Him in return. Does there need to be anything more to giving? It's an act of love.

Benefits of Giving

Do not judge, and you will not be judged. Do not condemn, and you will not be condemned. Forgive, and you will be forgiven.
—Luke 6:37

A lot of people don't give when the offering plate is passed around. Twenty percent of churchgoers make up those who provide most of the tithes and offerings.[8] Their reward will be commensurate with their giving. Don't be concerned about how much someone else gives. The heart of this passage is about how *you* give and God's response to you.

> *Give, and it will be given to you. A good measure, pressed down, shaken together and running over, will be poured into your lap. For with the measure you use, it will be measured to you.*
>
> **—Luke 6:38**

Money is not even mentioned in this verse. The lesson could be applied to anything, including your time, compassion, talents, food, and possessions. The principle is the same. How much you give affects how much you'll receive in return.

We see it in nature as well. Planting apple seeds, for example, will, in time, result in hundreds of apples filled with seeds that can be planted, and so on. You will always get more back than you could ever give. God cannot be outgiven!

But don't give just to get. That's the wrong motivation. Look at the widow's example. She gave because she loved the Lord, unlike the rich people, who gave to look good. Jesus was pleased with her. That was the attitude He was looking for.

While you probably are thinking about money when you read this passage in Luke, don't overlook its application to your conduct. If you condemn someone, you will be condemned. Forgiveness begets forgiveness. It's easy to see kindness returned when kindness is given. The bottom line is that you get what you give. If you give judgment, you'll get judgment in return.

The Right Heart

Give to everyone who asks you, and if anyone takes what belongs to you, do not demand it back....

And if you lend to those from whom you expect repayment, what credit is that to you? Even sinners lend to sinners, expecting to be repaid in full.

—Luke 6:30, 34

Give to others with no expectation of return. That is the heart of Jesus. That is what He would do. All giving should stay between the Lord and you. It is an act of love, quiet and intimate.

Jesus said that how you spend your time concerns Him as well:

Then the King will say to those on his right, "Come, you who are blessed by my Father; take your inheritance, the kingdom prepared for you since the creation of the world. For I was hungry and you gave me something to eat, I was thirsty and you gave me something to drink, I was a stranger and you invited me in, I needed clothes and you clothed me, I was sick and you looked after me, I was in prison and you came to visit me."

Then the righteous will answer him, "Lord, when did we see you hungry and feed you, or thirsty and give you something to drink? When did we see you a stranger and invite you in, or needing clothes and clothe you? When did we see you sick or in prison and go to visit you?"

The King will reply, "Truly I tell you, whatever you did for one of the least of these brothers and sisters of mine, you did for me."

—Matthew 25:34–40

You can easily become overwhelmed if you look at this parable as a to-do list, thinking that you must do all these things in order to please God. That is not the point. Again, this is a matter of the heart. When you see someone who is thirsty, give that person a drink. Do you know someone in prison? Go visit that person. Do you know someone who is sick? Offer to bring over soup and tea. Sick people need your care. Especially consider those who are home- or hospital-bound and unable to leave, such as the elderly, those who are terminally ill, and pregnant women on bed rest. They may need someone to sit with them as an encouraging presence so they know that they are not alone.

Life is truly short. You can waste the precious time you have been given on this earth on totally inconsequential things like smartphones and social media, or you can spend your fleeting life as a living expression of God's love.

There are people around you every day who need your time and concern. Love them, and you will be loving God as you do. Serve them, and you will be serving God as you do.

How to Become a Giver

How do you break the habit of not giving and become a giver?

Ask God for help. He is faithful to respond when we ask (Matthew 7:7–8).

Simply start tithing. It's simple to write a check or put money in the offering plate. It's an easy, clear symbol of giving to God. This act is a great way to see God's faithfulness to care for you, and then you'll find it easier to give in other areas of your life.

If you've been tithing your finances but not giving in any other area of your life, *look closely at your motives.* Why are you giving just a portion of your life to the Lord?

We've seen that He asks for all. Spend time with Him to ask how else you can give.

Be a giver rather than a taker. There are times when you have needs, but to take, take, take all the time reveals a close-fisted heart. Think about how you can use your time, talents, and money for Him. Like a seed that grows strong roots and perfect fruit, give. You won't regret it.

God wants all of you, from your talents to your agenda, from your time to your forgiveness of others. He loves you, and He desires your love in return.

> *For God so loved the world that he gave his one and only Son, that whoever believes in him shall not perish but have eternal life.*
> **—John 3:16**

The greatest gift ever given was God's Son, Jesus, who died for your sins. He held nothing back until the work for which He was sent was completed. Surrender is a radical concept, but total surrender will make you totally free. Jesus wants you to be a river of life poured out to the world, which He bought at such a high cost. He has planted good seed, nourished and cultivated your roots, given you the Holy Spirit, and supplied your every need. All He needs now is your surrender.

WORKBOOK

Chapter Seven Questions

Question: Other than money, what are some commodities that God wants you to give? In what areas do you find it most challenging to give?

_____

_____

_____

_____

_____

_____

_____

_____

_____

_____

Question: What advice about financial giving would you share with someone who is struggling to make ends meet? How can church leaders be sensitive toward those in need when they make appeals for necessary funding?

_____

_____

_____

_____

_____

_____

_____

_____

_____

_____

_____

Question: What heart attitudes should accompany giving? What attitudes suggest giving for the wrong reasons? The last time you gave, did you view it as a privilege, a duty, or a burden?

_____

_____

_____

_____

Action: Make a list of blessings that the Lord has given
you. Create a plan for one specific way you can give more
of your finances, time, and/or talents.

Chapter Seven Notes

_____

_____

_____

_____

_____

_____

_____

_____

_____

_____

_____

_____

_____

_____

_____

_____

_____

_____

_____

_____

CONCLUSION

Change the Harvest

Now that you have purified yourselves by obeying the truth so that you have sincere love for each other, love one another deeply, from the heart. For you have been born again, not of perishable seed, but of imperishable, through the living and enduring word of God. For, "All people are like grass, and all their glory is like the flowers of the field; the grass withers and the flowers fall, but the word of the Lord endures forever." And this is the word that was preached to you.

—1 Peter 1:22–25

Now that you've finished reading this book, you should have a better grasp of the principles that should be present in the life of a true believer. I have presented you with the standard. Now that you have a measuring stick, ask yourself whether you are actually living as a Christian instead of just saying that you're a Christian and living a worldly life. It is the deepest desire of my heart to see you set free, enjoying the fullness of life as a child of God.

You must separate from the world in order to be holy. Depend on Christ to help you walk into His holiness, for there are countless temptations out there that will throw you off the track. Spend time in the Word and in prayer and plant the right seeds so that your roots will be strong and your fruit will be sweet. If you're planting useless seeds, you'll only get useless fruit. However, you can change the harvest at any time by making the right choices and giving it time to grow. In the meantime, you can keep your joy as you trust God and wait for the new blessings to come.

Don't give in to a life of sin and selfishness. Praise God, have consistent devotions, avoid the lusts of the flesh, give freely of your resources and gifts, share your faith, and fellowship with other believers.

Be open to God and allow Him to speak to you. Your Christian walk will deepen and become more meaningful than it has ever been. Be a true believer. Determine to spend your life lavishly for Jesus. You will never regret it.

About the Author

A. Gilbert Ybarra and his wife, Fannie Ybarra, are the co-founders and Senior Pastors of The River of Life Christian Fellowship in Patterson, CA. He and his wife have been married for twenty-nine years (at the time this book was written), and together they have four grown children. Pastor Ybarra has been serving in ministry since the early age of fifteen. He received his undergrad degree in theology from Oral Roberts University and a master's degree in Biblical Studies from Liberty University. He is continuing his education and plans to receive his doctorate degree in the near future. Visit www.gilbertybarra.com to learn more.

REFERENCES

Notes

[1] Boom, Corrie ten, John Sherrill, and Elizabeth Sherrill. *The Hiding Place.* Chosen Books, 1971.

[2] Osteen, Joel. *Your Best Life Now: 7 Steps to Living at Your Full Potential.* Faithwords, 2004.

[3] Strong, James. "H7321 – ruwa`." *Strong's Exhaustive Concordance of the Bible.* Hunt & Eaton, 1894. In Blue Letter Bible. https://www.blueletterbible.org/lang/lexicon/lexicon.cfm?Strongs=H7321&t=KJV.

[4] "The Power of Worship and Praise." *Worship U.* Bethel Music. November 11, 2014. https://worshipu.com/testimony-worship-midst-crucible.

[5] George, Timothy. *Galatians.* Vol. 30, *The New American Bible Commentary.* Broadman & Holman, 1994, p. 400.

[6] Leaf, Caroline. *The Gift in You: Discovering New Life Through Gifts Hidden in Your Mind.* Inprov Ltd. (Kindle

Edition), locations 2079–2082.

[7] Graham, Billy. "A Daily Process – October 2." Billy Graham Evangelistic Association. https://billygraham.org/devotion/a-daily-process.

[8] Zylstra, Sarah Eekhoff. "Your Tithe Doesn't Have to Go to Your Church, Most Leaders Say: But for Many Christians, It May Be a Moot Point." Christianity Today. September 15, 2017. https://www.christianitytoday.com/news/2017/september/your-split-tithe-doesnt-have-to-go-to-church-ministries.html.